Slave Ship Earth
The Ultimate Triumph of Capitalism

I0493603

Bharat S. Shah, M.D.

Setubandh Publications
New York

The Slave Ship Earth:
The Ultimate Triumph of Capitalism
By Bharat S. Shah, M.D.

Price US $8.00

ISBN-13: 978-1499750348
ISBN-10:   149975034X

For a list of other books by the author
Please see the end pages

Preface

The capitalist system of economics has enjoyed an unparalleled and total success, and has virtually eradicated all threats from communism and socialism. It is embraced by western civilizations. However, other cultures perceive it as a harbinger of evil, while they would nonetheless love to have at least a part of all the comforts and leisure afforded by it.

Both the United States and Western Europe enjoy the fruits of capitalism, while its drawbacks are generally glossed over as the "price we pay." Concerns voiced by various nations of Asia and Africa are easy to dismiss as anti-modern bias, unfounded accusations or love for the status quo.

It is a risky business to point out anything wrong with capitalism, despite our constitutional guarantee of freedom of thought, expression, and belief. Any such imprudence is promptly met by cries of foul play, and is invariably labeled as "communism" or "socialism." Senator Joe McCarthy's ghost still hounds us.

It is difficult to understand why our nation, striving to achieve "a more perfect union" of its States, cannot accept even a likelihood of a "more perfect" economic system. Any hint of criticism of capitalism puts us on the offensive.

While the current work is certainly not a flowering tribute to the capitalist system, it is not an angry diatribe against it either. Its premise is simple: any system routed in a base human instinct like greed, is bound to be as imperfect as human beings, with room for perpetual improvement. The aim is to scrutinize the negatives to find anything that can be ameliorated to make capitalism more acceptable by those who are hesitant to embrace it now, and those who are suffering under it.

I have done that in the past, and have had published the "Capitalism, colonization of America, and the mating behavior of the praying mantis," in which only the effects of uncontrolled capitalism were described. The latter are not repeated here, except to synthesize them into a coherent whole and define the real problem on hand, rather than engaging in circular finger pointing.

As a Long Island doctor, my claim of being anti-capitalist, or anti-business can hardly be credible and indeed, I am neither of these. I am from a business community, and can claim to have a first hand knowledge of workings of a business. I am writing this out of concern for the business, capitalism, and for the America.

Any mention of the Native Americans, African Americans, and slavery, etc., is made to make a point, rather than to open up the sore wounds. Some faults may be uncovered, however, pointing out a perpetrator is not the purpose of this work.

I am not an economist, and I have read a handful of easy books on economics. After this book went to press, I have ordered and received books by Adam Smith, Karl Marks, F. A. Hayek, Thomas Picketty, and others, and have found them to be eminently awe inspiring, yet somewhat unreadable. I do plan to read them, have read a little bit already, but none of that reading has influenced this book, simply because their content needs to be digested.

This is not a scholarly work, therefore, it contains no references or footnotes. I have been observing the economic situation in the USA for the last several years with some bewilderment. I have been more and more dismayed that such a system can be tolerated at all by the American people. That made me go to the roots of the issues, and its outcome is this work.

As a physician, a healer, the present author can diagnose an ailment and offer treatment without being judgmental. He has no special expertise in economics, nor has he appeared as a talking head on any TV shows. He has been amply exposed to the vagaries of the capitalist and socialist systems. It is hoped that the reader will find this exercise interesting and worthwhile.

Since this is not a suspense thriller, a word about its title is in order. We are all slaves to our egos, desires, biases, delusions, and reluctance to think. Most often, we worship what we were born into, grew up with, or what we once fell in love with, no matter how untenable that position may be.

On the slave ships of the ante-bellum era, on their "middle passage," not only the unfortunate human cargo, but the captain and the crew all were sliding towards their slave lords. The proponent of capitalism, the one preaching it as a gospel, and the intended converts, all are slaves. That does not leave anyone out. Let us hope to find the right master.

I would like to thank my reviewers Nikhil, Hasmukh, Avani, Manisha, and Mr. Michael Buttenhauser for their valuable suggestions and comments.

Bharat S. Shah, M.D.
New York.
August 2014.

***

TABLE OF CONTENTS

Books by Bharat S. Shah, M.D.

***

Introduction

It is said, "Wealth is virtue," that is, if you have wealth, you apparently do not need any virtues. The latter is for the poor, or for those who are willingly happy to be so, or for those who are destined to be so. Wealth is power. Wars have been fought over wealth, wine, and women. The victor writes the history, and can claim to be virtuous.

Capitalism reigns supreme. Communism and its close relative socialism have fallen out of favor. Only the capitalist system of economics is said to be compatible with democracy. Communism is a dictatorship of the laborers and the Communist party, with no room for any dissent. Socialism is the dictatorship of the society as a whole, to which the individual has to defer.

Under capitalism, the individual is supreme. (S)he can posses wealth, property, and has a right to dissent. The latter automatically leads to a democratic system of government, since the right to dissent is meaningless without a forum in which to voice it and to redress it. Furthermore, as communism and socialism do not grant freedom of speech, expression, belief, and assembly, the democratic government and capitalist system are supposedly the best guarantors of these human rights.

Capitalism is based on human greed, providing motivation for hard work, efficiency, and productivity. Not everybody subscribes to this way of thinking. There are those who worship virtues, without necessarily being virtuous themselves. They abhor the idea of greed as the motivating force for human good.

Most religions consider greed to be a sin, indicating thereby that it is not beneficial to the society. On the contrary, what is good for a party or a class of the populace may not be perceived as being necessarily good for the individual.

Another crucial point is role of the government in guarding the common good, in providing municipal and health services, education, and in controlling the markets and the economy. Should it be allowed or required to protect or manipulate any of these? If yes, then under what conditions and restrictions can it do that? What about the government's freedom to act?

Since Communism is not compatible with democracy, despite all its claims to the contrary, one is automatically led to assume that Capitalism and democracy go hand in hand. We talk about exporting both to the third world simultaneously. We have to scrutinize this association thoroughly.

Assuming capitalism, or democracy, or both to be good for some countries, does it necessarily follow that they are good for the rest of the world? What agency of other countries will negotiate the deal? Can their governments surrender their peoples' interests and their own responsibilities to a foreign philosophy? If capitalism is granted a free rein, will it assume any responsibility? Who should monitor its compliance?

The current situation is in a flux, and answers to these and other questions may have to wait, but the questions themselves constitute the subject matter of the present work. They need to be discussed in an unbiased manner. Once we assume that something is true, we tend to selectively gather the evidence in its support. The burden of proof rests on the shoulder of a theory's proponents.

In other sciences, it is customary to use the null hypothesis, that any appearance of a pattern or a relationship is not valid, then try to show their validity, and thereby, essentially rejecting the null hypothesis. We will do this qualitatively by thinking through and discussing the issues, and leave it up to the reader to judge whether those assumptions are tenable and justifiable.

***

Capitalism and America

Although capitalism and America are considered synonymous today, capitalism in the USA is a relic from the colonial past. It was developed in France and England to protect the interests of the feudal lords. It had nothing to do with democracy, but rather to work in spite of it. England, France, Spain, and Portugal had colonies in Asia and Africa, and the Americas.

When the thirteen colonies won their independence, they began liberating also from anything that was British. The United States developed a different kind of democracy, different system of weights and measures, different kind of football, began to play baseball instead of cricket, and evolved its own American English language.

However, it forgot to get rid of the capitalist system of economy. The founding fathers did not find any reason to do away with that relic of foreign rule, maybe, because many of them were land lords of large estates, and could not think as serfs.

Understandably, President George Washington and others owned slaves, as was customary then. Jefferson and others tried unsuccessfully to abolish slavery, as the latter was incompatible with any desire for freedom, but had to give in to demands of the Southern States to be. Capitalist interests prevailed over a newborn, or an yet unborn democracy.

Capitalism Since the Birth of America

When the Pilgrims landed in America, they had to survive against the natural calamities, and against the native population. Gradually, the latter was reduced to oblivion, and pushed into the Indian lands. William Penn established better relationship with the Indians, and created a harmonious haven, today's Pennsylvania. In the rest of the country, the Indians survived as names of sport teams like Cleveland Indians, or Washington Redskins. They also survived in names of rivers like Connecticut, and cities like Poughkeepsie.

(A.) *The American Indians and the European arrivals*

The Native Americans used bow and arrows for weapons, and the canoe for transport of goods. Horse was their land vehicle and the beast of burden. They could forge metal into arrows and ornaments. Their own muscles provided energy. The pilgrims brought larger and better ships, and gunpowder.

Everybody had to work manually, and the work was hard. All agricultural and manufacturing activities required lot of muscle power. Some jobs demanded more skills than others. The harder one worked, the higher were the rewards. There was plenty of land to be owned, occupied, and to be cultivated. The country gradually expanded from "the sea to shining sea."

With increasing population and limited habitable land, some people were unable to own sufficient land or their own business. They had to work for others and were paid for their labors. The population was still relatively homogeneous, but young and energetic. The gap between owners and laborers was small, and the line of separation permitted two-way traffic with great ease. Gambling, alcohol, and speculation were gradually creeping in.

Earning one's daily bread and being reasonably happy was not difficult. However, that is not the way to be wealthy. Being rich is generally a zero-sum game. Riches cannot exist without poverty. Among the rich also, some may be more so than others, and both of them can pass as rich, if the zero-sum game is expanded to larger population and other nations.

Obtaining resources and energy from abroad was not easy then, for the world had yet to shrink. Labor could be imported, or rather, laborers could be imported, but that would increase the population desirous of sharing the same dream of getting rich.

(B.) Slavery, and the Human Beast

This is a painful and embarrassing topic; yet, it cannot be wished away or omitted from this narrative. Last year, I visited the Schaumberg Center of Black History, in the Harlem area of the New York City. Anybody who thinks (s)he knows all there is to know about the black history and slavery may do well to pay it a visit.

While there, I bought maybe, 10-12 books by various black and non-black writers, poets, and historians, not to leave out the firebrands like Malcolm-X, and educationist like Booker T. Washington. There were speeches by women like Sojourner Truth.

There was one relatively large book by Ms. Harriet Washington, called "The Medical Apartheid." It detailed the treatment of the blacks by the medical profession from before the Civil War (the *ante-bellum* period) through the 1990s. Yes, the 1990s. I read it from cover to cover, including notes and references, with tears in one eye, and blood running from my other, a doctor's eye.

Other books backed up the evidence provided by Ms. Washington, and documented the human element, the anguish, and helplessness matched by callousness. We will return to its content later, but what struck me like a stone on my head, was that it was not only a history. If it was, then it was being perpetually repeated as current events.

My eyes popped out when I saw the aftermath of God being replaced by greed. Plantation-owners, the medical profession, the Christian Church, and the local and the Federal Governments, all joined unwittingly to annihilate an entire race, which was Christian, and many of its members were born in the USA.

We will not dwell on this shameful part of the American history. Not that it is unimportant, but because it requires and deserves more extensive treatment. Here, we will touch it from the economic point of view.

Imported laborers offered many advantages. They were not just laborers, but were slaves. They were bought and sold like a commodity. They neither had to be paid for their work, nor to be provided for, nor cared for, except just enough to keep them working. The slave women could be impregnated and bred like cattle, and be slaughtered at will. Once grown up, their children could be sold, too.

Another advantage of having slaves over the animals was that slaves could be taught to operate tools and use their hands somewhat skillfully. Once broken in, they can spontaneously do additional work for their master's family, taking care of masters' women and children. When their masters went to battle the Lincoln's Union army, to preserve slavery, the very slaves protected the masters' family, and took care of the wounded master on his return.

Unlike the local workers, the slaves did not deserve to have a vacation, or a sick leave. Not that they did not fall ill, but when they did, their symptoms were attributed to laziness and tactics to avoid working. They were whipped back to work or to die. Replacing a slave was the most cost efficient action.

(C.) Industrialization

The industrial revolution of the nineteenth century changed the lot of the slaves, at least in Europe and in the northern United States. Machines were more productive, and offered fewer problems, moral, ethical, and humanitarian. But machines were expensive, there were up front costs, and they were expensive to repair when they broke down. Replacement parts and downtime increased the costs and decreased the profits.

It is not necessary to rehash the events leading to and through the Civil War and the subsequent Emancipation of the slaves. Nothing changes overnight, especially if it offers some special benefits to a select and powerful group.

Human conscience cannot be legislated. Even though rape and murder are illegal, they continue to occur.

Slaves became free without knowing how to handle their new freedom and shoulder their new responsibilities, even if they knew what those were. They were illiterate, and were not skilled enough to manage a plantation or another business. Their poverty, unemployment, criminal activities, drinking, and apparent loose morals increased. They had no legal rights to complain or to bear a witness. Imprisonment for crimes, real and imagined, public lynching, and other predicaments continued.

Industrialization made the Emancipation inevitable, however, further industrialization was to make those slaves and many more of the population fall slaves to the machines. Furthermore, the electronic revolution and the advent of the robotics were to make the human labor superfluous, within a century or so.

Hundred years after the Civil War and the Emancipation, Rev. Martin Luther King, Jr. had to lead the March on Washington for the civil rights of the Blacks. More than fifty years after that, we have a Black President who is not immune from racially motivated abuse either. He has been accused of trying to redistribute the wealth, a deadly sin against capitalism.

The word "accused" is a fantastic invention. It can transform a virtue into a vice. One can be accused of being chaste, honest, empathetic, or decent, and thereby be shamed to death. The wealthy feel threatened by any attempt to narrow the gap between them and the poor, even though the threat is more perceived and rather imaginary than real. It is also more a remote possibility than an imminent one.

It should not come as a surprise to know that fear and power go hand in hand, and one leads to the other. You cannot afford to tolerate a hole in a massive dam, you see! Fear forces one to amass wealth and power, and once acquired, the latter generates the fear of losing it.

When the Northern States became industrialized, they had little difficulty in living without their slaves. The plantations also could have been industrialized, but they found it too difficult to live without the cheap and renewable free labor that the slaves offered. The machines provided relief from human torture. The North welcomed that relief, since Canada and European nations had done away with slavery altogether.

New inventions and the means of production were coming rapidly. Machines were providing more free time and goods were getting cheaper, thanks to mass production. Industrial progress manifested in the form of the skies over the cities filling up with smoke and smog, rivers becoming sewers, and cities filling up with ghettos. Already, some thinkers had begun to worry about dehumanization caused by the machines.

Human beings that once replaced the animals, and then freed by machines, were now put in the service of the machines, to work on the assembly lines, and to live in dark quarters with no amenities to speak of. Newly freed but illiterate and isolated slaves became free, to work voluntarily on the same plantations. Those who migrated to towns and cities had a change of masters, but of practically nothing else.

(D.) Women and the Wars

The captive women slaves had the worst fate. They were used as breeding machines, impregnated by their masters or by another slave at the whim of the masters. Even they got the citizenship and voting rights with the Emancipation.

But, not all slaves were captured and kidnapped, not all are Black either. Today, many white "slaves" are married to their "masters." Power subsists on slavery of one kind or the other. Through the time immemorial, women have been treated ruthlessly as slaves, by their men.e freedmen Blacks were granted citizenship and a right to vote. However, the *white* women had no right to vote, even though they were citizens of the USA. They did have the right to suffer, but no suffrage was granted to them. Even to date, in some parts of the world, women have been kept illiterate, have been forbidden to venture out, to move around and mingle freely, or to hold office. Chivalry can shroud slavery, too.

If women started working in offices, factories, and the corporate boardrooms, that would dilute the work force and lower the remuneration for everybody. Since women are duty bound to their households, children, and families, are considered feeble, in need for protection, and are emotionally too labile to hold responsible offices, have bad habit of getting pregnant and staying away from work, therefore, they should be kept away from the man's domain. It would be good for all, or so the thinking went.

Two world wars with associated loss of "man" power, either deployed, permanently lost abroad, opened up the inevitable door for women to move in. Soon enough, a homemaker woman almost became an anomaly. It took the

Civil War to liberate the slaves, but the world wars to liberate women.

The rationale for disqualifying women from the work force was, they were supposedly emotional, not always logical, feeble, and not wise enough to be permitted to share an equal status with men. To recall, the slaves were also said to be of inferior breed, genetically deficient, lacking intelligence, and fit only to serve their masters. Just as keeping slaves can further your prosperity, marrying the rich "slaves" was the surest way to gain it, in Victorian England.

The Blacks gained the voting right before women did. Now we already have a Black President, can a woman be far behind? What does all this have to do with capitalism? Well, the Blacks were not permitted to have any property, and had no rights even over their own bodies. Women have had no identity, separate from that of their fathers and husbands. In many parts of the world, they had no right to property or inheritance. Very few had credit history of their own. Such inequalities lead to exploitation and dependence, and a vicious cycle is set in motion.

(E.) Immigrants

Unlike the Blacks and the women in the USA, immigrants lack the US citizenship, and officially, they cannot have certain rights and benefits. People from the world over have migrated to America in search of their dreams, the least of which is to make a living. Irish and other Europeans, Jewish people, and recently Africans and Asians have come, too. Political refugees also find asylum here.

America is a nation of immigrants, and both have helped each other. Many, if not most, immigrants come with only a few pennies in their pockets, and then earn their way to prosperity, depending upon their educational and other backgrounds. Just like women and Blacks, they are paid at lower rate, much lower, since the minimum wage laws or Union protection they do not have.

We know why they cannot go back to their country of origin. There are no jobs, while in America, under the capitalist system, the production of goods has increased, so is the demand for them, and hence, more workers are needed. The capitalist lords are the job creators, and they throw pittance at their laborers who can better their lots, far more rapidly than was possible ever before. This is the "trickle down theory" by which the workers' living standard is lifted. Be it as it may, but it does tickle up their fancy and raise their hopes and expectations.

Even though less than what they expect or deserve, they make more than what they could ever make back home, if they could find a job there at all. Many are undocumented or illegal aliens, and are afraid to be caught by the immigration officers and be deported. They are in no position to stand up for their rights, even if they knew what they were. The immigrants have left their mother countries on their own, maybe, reluctantly or under duress, but there is no going back. They tend to put up with come what may.

Many immigrants live in ghettos of their own creation. They huddle together to gain emotional support, familiar surroundings, and stepping-stones to ease themselves into at least the fringes of the main stream. They can be exploited, cheated, threatened with being reported and deported, and can be hushed up. If this creates a condition not unlike slavery, at least it is voluntary. Just because it is voluntary, it cannot be disqualified from being slavery.

(F.) The Mexican Immigrants

The immigrants from across the border to the south are a special case. They can come here legally like any other immigrants. Some are smuggled in from far-off countries via Mexico. A great majority are Mexican day laborers coming to work in farms and fields of Texas and California. Some of them literally commute if that is possible, while others stay for a week or two at a time, and some, much longer.

Entire towns of Mexico near the border with the US depend up on income from these laborers. Closing the border has not proved very practical for a nation of immigrants, and for the local farmers and others dependent upon their cheap labor. Their employers like to enjoy the fruits of their labor, but cannot stand to have them obtain any benefits in return. Basic services like health care or schooling are not to be offered to laborers settled for long haul. They have to return to Mexico, should they need to use the toilet, it seems.

(G.) Doctors and Other Professionals

In the mid 1960s, the immigration opened up for professionals, bringing in a huge influx of doctors, engineers, and other professionals. The World War II, the Korean War, and The Vietnam War had created a shortage of doctors on the home front, and increased demands for medical care at the same time. New technologies and new expertise were in demand.

To compound the problem, the organized medicine had kept the number of seats in medical schools, and residency staff positions in hospitals low. Most of these were in the well to do areas of the city. The inner city public hospitals serving the poor did not have enough physicians. The latter communities prevailed up on the Congress to open up the immigration for the foreign doctors.

The physicians from Canada and Europe were always welcome, but they were not desperate to come here. Instead, the Asians came in droves. They were welcome by the poor, totally deprived of medical care, while hated by the organized medicine.

They came from the same countries from which a few decades hence, students were going to excel in the American schools, take over the spelling bees, and science talent searches, and the Microsoft and other tech businesses were to appeal to the government to open the doors wider for letting their engineers in.

American medicine started a campaign to make the alien doctors' life miserable. It was quite experienced at that, because it had done the same to keep women, Blacks, and Jews away from medicine, and had done the same to the Homeopaths and Chiropractors, while befriending the Osteopaths.

Complex network of exams and licensing requirements were put in place, and a systematic slander campaign was set in motion. The foreign medical graduates (FMG) were described as poorly trained, speaking bad English, even though most were trained with British books and had studied medicine in English as medium of instruction.

Many accusations were leveled at us, including being "quitters," "uncaring desrters of their motherlands," unable to pasas the US exams," "without US licenses to practice medicine (only the US citizens were allowed to take the exmas," and so on. My favorite of all the accusations levied against us was,"Off the many who tried to come to the US, only a few were able to make it." That should have pleased the organized medicine, but it did not.

Using their logic, or rather the lack of it, one can say that the Presidents of the US are no good because most of those who aspire to become one never make it! The FMGs who had come to the US were being blamed for those who did not make it. This is the best example of logic of a scientific community whose thinking is guided by greed alone. Money talks, and people listen, even if the talk is nonsense.

Some US born students had gone to offshore medical schools. They were US-born citizens. Even then, they were required to demonstrate their proficiency in English (their mother tongue) by passing the Test for English as a Foreign Language (TOFEL). English was not a foreign language for them.

Many had already obtained graduate and post-graduate degrees from prestigious colleges. One such student (USFMG) had done his Masters in Biology from the New York University before doing medicine from an offshore med school. He had to clear the TOEFL before being accepted into a residency program in the US!

The FMGs worked where American doctors would not care to or dare to go. In the early days of the AIDS epidemic, FMGs provided care in the poor public hospitals overflowing with terminal AIDS patients who were of the same age as the FMGs treating them. The slander and obstructionism continued.

Spouses of FMGs were not permitted to work. Many of these spouses were doctors or other professionals. Many of them got trapped in the web of innumerable exams, got frustrated, and abandoning medicine, opened provision stores, or motels, or obtained work as taxi drivers, elevator operators, or night watchmen (most spouses were women). Meanwhile, Nurses and even less trained people were being recruited as Physicians' Assistants to relieve doctors of their heavy burden without threatening their income.

A Threat to Capitalism:

Capitalism thrives on competition. Any time, the free flow of competition is blocked by artificially created borders and boundaries to keep a selected group's income safe, while preventing others, especially of different race, or of different national origin, from gaining access to practice of the professional. The Immigration Department can take care of such inflow, but others have no right to take over its job.

"Treatment" of the Blacks:

Let us return to the way in which the Blacks were treated over the years. It is beyond the scope of this work to detail the abuses of Blacks completely, but they were subjected to experiments under the guise of "treatment," that was never given, even when something went wrong. Blacks never got the benefits of the so-called therapies, even when they worked, but were rather given to the "superior" race. Major medical centers in New York were involved in this. Those who want to learn about this shabby period, should read Ms. Harriet Washington's book, "The Medical Apartheid."

(H.) What is Common among the FMGs, Blacks, Slaves, and Women?

They were all treated the same way. There was a difference in the degree and in the severity, of the abuse they were subjected to, but the tactics and techniques employed were the same, adapted to the situation on hand.

Capitalism thrives on profit and greed. Cheap and captive labor is welcome, as long as there is nothing to be paid in return. No benefits, meager pay —if any at all — and no opportunity to become a challenge in the future.

The latter requires some justification to make it presentable, and to clear the conscience or whatever of that is left behind. They are all supposedly inferior, feeble, poorly trained, not appropriate for the job, just hungry vultures, lazy misfits, good for nothing, fit only to be subservient to the masters.

That is the common thread running through all these problems or issues. As if the *masters* had the slavery "issue," while slaves were having all the fun, *they* had the FMG "problem," while the FMGs were sucking all the blood out. It appears that blaming the victims, defaming them, slandering them, and humiliating them to make them thankful for whatever is thrown at them, has always been the game.

Taking full advantage of the helplessness of the admittedly weak, feeble, poor, untrained, with poor command of language were not going to be offered any special training, support, or teaching. That would be counter-productive, inefficient, and would go against the maximization of their profits.

Only the properties can appreciate, people should never be. It did not matter that plantations could not survive without the slave labor, or that many jobs would have gone unfilled without women, or that there would have been no medical care in the inner-city areas without the FMGs. Still, the capitalist interests lobbied the government to pass restrictive laws that were only in their own interests, against those of the populace at large. Greed does not have to be pro-America, but only pro-oneself, and the government of the people, by the people, and for the people does not have to be pro-people either.

Even in the grammar, we talk about the future of the past tense, and the past form of the future tense. Similarly, the history cannot be considered in distinct slabs or layers of time-periods. History is an on-going process, and remnants of the past can coexist with the present. The events and problems seem to recede into background when we stop talking about them, but they do not necessarily disappear. Slavery, the FMG problem, and the women's liberation are such entities. They have reached a detent with the history.

***

Some Asects of the Capitalism

1. Free-Market Economy

Capitalism requires and runs on free-market economy, free from controls and interference by governments and other regulations. The colonization did provide this quite well, although the colonies lost their voice in any of these. So, the freedom is for the capitalist, who can then deprive others of that. As we saw, the laborers from Africa and Asia do not have a free access to the capitalist factories in the countries of Europe and America.

This one-sided freedom is understandable and excusable, since the capitalist system never claimed to be an altruistic, international, humanitarian entity. It was after all, meant to serve the interests of a particular country and its businesses. Unfortunately for them, the middle of the twentieth century saw a severe erosion of colonization, especially the direct, political, and military colonization.

The colonies that were exploited until now, became independent, but with all their businesses and technological infrastructure in the ruins. They thought that their salvation lay with the capitalist system that they also could now exploit to their advantage. They were no different than the emancipated slaves, and their actions were similar as well.

They sought to become prosperous by selling their raw materials at yet lower prices to their once colonial lords, voluntary colonization, if you will, and a subtle one at that. Colonies like the USA were in a better shape. Their colonization was not deep rooted, and was thrown over rather at a young age. Their capitalist businesses did not have to colonize distant lands for obtaining raw materials. They had them aplenty in the new world.

Growing population provided ever-growing new markets, reinforced by planned obsolescence of merchandize. The USA was a unique, self-sufficient colony. It did not have to exploit other far away countries to sustain its capitalist pursuits.

2. Maximization of Profits

Businesses given a free rein, unencumbered by myriad regulations, can concentrate on maximizing the production of goods, at highest efficiency, and thereby maximizing profits. This "maximization" is a lovely term that has attracted a very large, but generally blind following.

As a medical student, I had studied Anatomy and Physiology. Before that during the pre-med years, I had been exposed to Biology of plants and animals. Growing up in a developing country like India, I had spent hours and days observing the cows grazing in dry pastures. Yet, I felt at a loss, when it came to appreciating the maximization. It just does not generally occur in the nature. Where it does occur, it is frowned up on as a destructive force.

When a cow grazes in the meadows, it bites off little bit of grass from here and there, constantly moving to different areas. It does not create a bald patch, devoid of all grass. The sheep are a different story. They denude the grassland, and encourage its erosion during subsequent rains. Therefore, sheep grazing is fought with tooth and nails, but not the cow grazing.

When the blood leaves our lungs after picking up oxygen, it carries 20 ml oxygen in 100 ml of blood. When it delivers oxygen to the tissues, it does not give up all its oxygen, not even most of it either. The venous blood still carries 15-16 ml of oxygen, that is, 75% of the Oxygen comes back unchanged to the heart and the lungs. The difference between the arterial and the venous blood (A-V O_2 difference) is only 4-5ml, or 25% of the maximum.

During my research on removing carbon dioxide from the blood of patients with emphysema (see "Questions, Answers, and Exclamations," in the end pages), I learned that removing all carbon dioxide from blood was damaging to the blood. In the open-heart surgery also, they blow in 5% carbon dioxide to prevent the washout of carbon dioxide.

Mother nature is not greedy, and she does not believe in maximization. She works with abundance and abandon. She gives an infinite rate of return on investment, not a meager 10-15%. Nature creates the golden-egg-laying hen. Those who "maximize," end up killing it. The maximization is for the poor and misers. It goes with capitalism. It may be bad for everybody else, and hence, bad for you, too.

Maximizing production drains resources, which is not a problem if there are inexhaustible supplies. Inexpensive labor when extended indefinitely, leads to slavery. Mass production with machines lowers the prices, unless the goods can be moved to new markets. In the post-colonial era that is not easy.

The old markets can be exploited maximally to act as new ones. Marketing and advertising lead to increased demands. Newer, better, different products may entice more buyers. Improvements, ease of use, and easy payment terms can facilitate more sales. Disposable items create a perpetual market.

So far so good, but when all businesses start using these tactics, competition becomes cut throat, benefitting the consumer. A company has to come up with really better and cheaper products, with major investment in research and development, which can lead to many dead ends, thereby raising costs and cutting into profits.

Consumerism just described is at the core of capitalism. Rapid turnover of goods and money feeds transport companies, sales staff, customer service, and many other intermediaries, thereby providing many jobs. These businesses are the job creators for the masses here and abroad.

3. Stock Market

Business owners invest their money to make profit. The lower the cost to produce the merchandise, and the higher the price, mean higher profit.

Costs include the money paid for raw materials, labor, machinery, energy, research and development, and on and on. Many of these are unpredictable, uncontrollable, or both.

Even with machines around, businesses need lot of employees to acquire materials, manufacture products, then market and sell them. These are personnel costs. Included in these are costs of vacations, sick leaves, the Social Security contributions, unemployment insurance, health insurance, and retirement plans.

The sale depends up on consumer preferences based on many factors, including some fickle ones. Looking at this grossly incomplete list of expenses, it is a surprise that businesses make any profit at all. Plus there are taxes to pay, and innumerable regulations to adhere to.

Owners do get to keep the rest of the profits. When thinking about owners, some very rich people, driving fancy and expensive cars, and living in huge mansions come to mind. However, many big businesses belong to people like you and me. We can buy stocks of that company, and expect to get our share of profits.

If people buy shares of a company, its value goes up, and the other way around. This is where the Wall Street and the Main Street meet. While ordinary people may collectively hold a large part of the total investment, usually the giant investment firms, banks, insurance companies, and pension plans run the show. Therefore, the Main Street component is generally ignored.

All the above forces come together to determine the price of a company's stock by a process akin to the parlor game of Ouija Board, and our collective judgment, and often the lack of it, moves the stock price higher or lower.

4. Anti-consumer Movement

The culture of disposable products at the cost of natural resources is called Consumerism, and the move to oppose that wasteful practice is known as Anti-Consumerism. Here, I am referring to a new phenomenon, wherein the companies cultivate and display an attitude that antagonizes their consumers. A business doing that to its consumers was inconceivable until now.

We saw how costs can be cut by employing free or cheap labor, and by exploiting colonies for their raw materials and buying power. In self-sufficient nations like the USA, the choice by the consumers can make or break a product and a company. Wooing the consumer is of great importance.

Wooing by an inapt suitor can lead to an unfortunate outcome. Trying to win sales by manipulating and exploiting consumer psychology to the extreme can lead to deception, cheating, and anti-consumer attitude, or killing the proverbial golden-egg-laying hen. Some of this is intentional and well planned.

We are not talking about various scams, like Ponzi schemes, and other criminal acts. There are many schemes that exist just to rip off consumers, or so it seems. Exorbitant pricing of hearing aids, and of dental implants are the best examples of "what the market can bear." Another racket is that of the time-shares. I have yet to hear of anyone who has sold his or her time-share unit and made a profit.

The frequent-flyers programs and various miles programs from the airlines or from the credit card companies generally exist to make consumers suffer.

The free overseas tickets keep on receding as the value of one's accrued miles keep decreasing.

The telephone bills of thousands of dollars from a non-scrupulous overseas company, has to be simply paid up, because the local phone company "collects the bills," but cannot do anything about it. We can bomb any part of the world to protect "our interests," we can invade Grenada "protect our few medical students," but cannot do anything to these crooks.

Have you noticed that the one-pound cans of products have lost weight and instead of 16 oz, they weigh 14 or 12 oz? Have you recently tried to squeeze a tube of toothpaste to see a large amount of air come out? The net weight is accurately printed, but the tube is made to look larger.

You may have thought that you have outsmarted the companies by buying a two-pound container rather than two of one pound each. Did you notice that the larger package costs more? Try to buy one banana at the price, two for 59 cents. You may pay 60 cents for one banana.

Now it is possible to fight the City Hall and win, but not so with the banks, and credit card companies. Have you not yet gotten sore fingers and aching ears in trying to resolve a customer service complaint? Is it not common to find out that your final payment is 25% higher than what you had computed?

In a capitalist society, one would think the consumer to be its sacred pillar. It has been said that the consumer is always right. Also, an educated customer is the best consumer. Customer Service and Consumer Satisfaction were buzzwords.

Not anymore. Just as a woman today does not have to marry a man to have a baby, businesses do not have to woo a consumer at all. The latter has become a commodity or worse, a nuisance, giving hard times to businesses they were supposed to make profitable, saving their money rather than spending to get the economy going.

If Consumers buy the goods, that helps. If they do not, they are useful to corporations and their CEOs (Chief Executive Officers) in other ways. They can be thrown overboard to lighten the load. This will make more sense if we remember that just like jobs and goods, consumers are also creation of the business. Employees of one business are consumers of another. When sales go down, employees become dead weight, and are let go. What is lost in sales is made up in personnel costs.

The problem of lost profit caused by thus lost consumers remains to be handled. A shrewd businessperson knows how to convert a problem into an opportunity. Decreasing the personnel costs is the simplest way to tilt the balance towards black. Every dollar thus saved, converts dollar for dollar into profit

To make do the same amount of work with fewer people and less cost is called efficiency. The workplace can be made progressively more efficient by compelling the remaining staff to absorb more work, or meet the same fate as that of their now ex-colleagues. Unions can be hushed up by threatening them with out-sourcing.

This profitability is achieved without developing any new or better product, without wasting money on research and development, or marketing and advertising, or opening up new markets. Consumers do not come in the picture at all. No customer service burden is incurred. Everybody loses, but the CEO, who is rewarded for raising the stock prices by his efficient handling of the situation. The shareholders are delighted, even though some of them may have been laid off.

Consumers Protection Bureau or Agency of the government is always under attack from the companies. The Consumers Advocate has the muscle that the consumers lack. Getting rid of the Consumers Advocate is cost-effective for the greedy and ruthless companies.

***

Colonization of America

For manufacturing any goods, one needs raw material, energy, and labor. The latter two can combine, or be separate. Raw materials are needed to produce the goods from them. The colonization of Asia, Africa, and Americas by the European countries was necessitated by shortage of raw materials. Also, the colonies provided new and captive markets for the abundant goods produced, even though the colonies may not have any need for them. They had to let go of the raw materials, which they themselves were capable of processing. Their businesses died.

America did not establish colonies, because it had enough land, inexhaustible resources, and few people. The founding fathers who were landlords themselves, kept the capitalist system, while discarding everything else that was British. As the population grew to fill the land, and the danger of dwindling resources was appreciated, the anti-consumer behavior appeared on the scene, and "protecting America's interests abroad" was felt necessary. Before that, America itself had to be controlled and conquered.

America was coming of age, and its people were working hard to obtain some benefits from the progress made. Environmental regulations and standards were eating away profits while the government was responding to the public outcry. Minimum wage laws and union benefits were making the situation worse.

The newly introduced Medicare, Medicaid, and the G.I. Bill, were taking money away from farm and tobacco subsidies. Alcohol, tobacco, guns and other firearms, and the defense equipment manufacturing came to fore front as new and lucrative products.

Medical research and the big pharmaceutical companies claimed a big chunk of money. The Social Security and Supplemental Security Income (SSI) for the middle class and the poor had to compete with the private interests. The government was interfering too much to be tolerated, the big business thought.

The intervention by the government had to stop. Since the government is for, of, and by the people, the people should go as well. Poverty was a drain on profits, so that had to go, too. The best way to get rid of the poverty is to get rid of the poor.

As the saving and loan debacle demonstrated, and as was seen during the housing mortgage crisis, debt finance stand off and the government shutdown, the government should save all its might to bail out the banks rather than the people. Banks were to big to fail, people were too small to be saved.

Government should take care of the mentally and physically ill, if they cannot pay. It should also take care of prisons and jails, unless that can be made profitable, and hence, privatized. The postal service should be compelled to put aside billions of dollars to cover its pension plans, even when no one else is required to. The FedEx can deliver letters, while the UPS can deliver parcels, and charge extra for Saturday delivery, or residential delivery, but the postal service cannot.

The capitalists want to have all rights and protections, but no responsibility. By now, we know the reason. They are the self-appointed captains of ship. They should be protected at the cost of everybody else. Was that not the rule of the sea? Profits before people, or rather, give them people and they will convert them into profits.

Lately, we have heard a lot about India and China snatching over our jobs. They come to the US in some space ships in the dark of the night, set up booths in major cities, and sweep up all the unfilled jobs — created by our job creators — and disappear before the day break.

Sending jobs abroad may have started as a way to avail oneself of the inexpensive raw materials and labor in the third world countries. Even after the freight charges, the goods manufactured abroad were cheaper, and more profitable.

The outsourcing eventually degenerated into a weapon to threaten the employees and keep their unions in their place. By declaring their own independence, the 1% converted America into their mere colony to be exploited at will, with nothing to offer in return, feeling no shame.

Our job creators did not create jobs in the numbers that were needed, plus, outsourced many more. Unemployment is an integral part of capitalism, however, the latter would just acknowledge this fact, without assuming any responsibility to address it.

No real gentleperson would want others to do what they did not want to do. The government should not be bothered with creating jobs. It creates useless and unproductive jobs, we are told. The government has to pay the unemployment benefits, and finds it cheaper to create jobs, hire people, and generate some tax revenue, saving on the unemployment benefits at the same time.

If the unemployed are worth their salt, they will find jobs soon enough. If they cannot, they are lazy, not motivated, uninterested, and in any case, undeserving of the benefits (Sounds familiar?). The unemployment payoffs should stop within a few months. That is how the theory goes.

If "they" do not create any jobs, do not let the government do that either, and insist on cutting the unemployment benefits, then we can see a solution to the problem of joblessness. Kill the unemployed or help them do it themselves. Poverty can be solved in the same way.

The gigantic multinational corporations wield a lot of power, and they do not hesitate to use it for their own good. They can lobby and tangle up the legislation, or can buy out the candidates. Our concern here is, they can thwart the competition that is the hallmark of capitalism. They become, effectively, monopolies, reminiscent of the State monopolies of Europe around the World War II, and if unchecked, pose a danger to capitalism itself.

5. Healthcare

Government should not get into the healthcare business, and it has no business getting into people's health insurance needs. If I were a capitalist, I would have loved the Obamacare which would have insured 40 million more people, giving business to insurance companies, and others. Apparently, there are some other sinister factors at play in the fight against the Obamacare, and we will leave it there.

The resistance, or sheer non-cooperation of some Southern States to expand Medicaid, even if the government would pay for them for the first three years, appears to be obstructionism, callousness, and a plan to force the poor (Blacks) out of those states.

Medical drugs and devices are getting to be unaffordable. All new developments in technology are raising the costs. No attempt is made towards decreasing them. Thousand-dollars-a-day drug for treating hepatitis: C is in the market. Artificial knees and hips cost several times more in the US than in other countries.

These drugs and devices can be made much cheaper in other countries, but there are issues of intellectual property rights, and quality control, are raised. Just as slander of migrants was used to stir up fear of imagined catastrophes in people's minds, slander of foreign companies making drugs and devices ensued, some well deserved, others not. There is no reason why the foreign companies cannot be ruthless in search of profits.

Intellectual right to property is used to maximize profits at the cost of human lives. Government and health insurers are blackmailed into paying whatever the drug manufacturers would demand. Again, government should not interfere, but just pay off and shut up. Any inventor should have a right to make money on his or her inventions, but the inventor gets hardly anything. Companies own their patents.

Attempts by the Obama administration to curtail costs by establishing a single party payment system for health care were thwarted. Now the fee-for-service way of paying will increase the costs, which can be blamed on the Obamacare.

Cost of research for new drugs and devices are said to be exorbitant, but no research is done to find cheaper remedies. If a drug is toxic beyond a certain arbitrary point, that drug is not approved. If it is toxic or even lethal to the pockets of the people or of their government, it is released anyway.

Most new drugs do not represent a true or major advance, but only a minor change in its formula here and there. Lot of money is spent in marketing and advertising their miniscule benefits. Research costs are business expenses to be born by the companies. They may be gradually passed on to the consumers, but not as an avalanche.

The capitalists want to keep the government out of everything, except to be there to pay them whatever and whenever they demand. It should stand at full attention to protect their property rights abroad and block the competition. It should be ready and willing to accept the blame for failing to do anything that the companies did not let the government do in the first place.

"Saving people's lives" and fear of "rationing the health care" are their buzzwords. They want to save peoples' lives by killing them with costs, and thwarting the health care rationing by making the care unaffordable. Fighting all attempts at controlling costs of treatments, or of establishing a one-payer system are their tactics.

6. Control of the Government

Keeping the number of workers low, keeping them under control by various means, keeping unions at bay, extorting exorbitant prices for drugs and devices, and keeping the government away except to write a check, go a long way towards assuring profits. However, an untamed government can do lot of damage to the capitalist agenda.

The government needs to be stopped before it can do anything to help people by lowering prices, or by protecting jobs or providing unemployment benefits. It has to be muzzled, stifled, and manipulated into inaction or nearly so.

The Legislative, and the Executive branches can be controlled by channeling the campaign contributions, lobbying, and by frightening the voters of an undesirable Congressman or a Senator. The fourth estate or the media can be either purchased outright, or through buying advertising. Some of these may be quite acceptable under a democratic system.

Outsourcing of jobs and manufacturing abroad offers the increased profits by lowering the costs with the lax regulations of toxic waste, poor worker-protection laws, and non-existent or poorly enforced child-labor laws. Outsourcing is an effective weapon to threaten rebellious workers and their unions with layoffs, and to make them accept poorer contracts.

Goods produced by American companies abroad are brought back to the States as "export," thereby affecting the balance of trade unfavorably. Overseas subsidiaries provide excellent camouflage for tax evasion. In this manner, the nation loses jobs, gets poor quality goods, gets bad name abroad, loses tax revenue, and incurs a negative balance of trade.

Companies do not pay taxes abroad either, and may get favorable tax breaks from foreign governments. For bringing that money home, they insist on getting tax amnesty from the US government. Remember that John Doe or Jane Doe does not get any amnesty when (s)he brings the pay check home. (S)he pays taxes even on the Social Security contributions that (s)he does not even bring home, and pays the income tax again when (s)he collects the benefits at age 65 or later.

Moreover, these companies use their carrots and sticks both to compel the government to use its powers via the World Bank and International Monetary

Fund to serve their own interests. They also look up to the government to provide help against foreign goods by levying tariffs on them. All this is obtained without doing anything at all for the government or the people of the USA.

At home, their lobbies like those of tobacco, guns, weapons, liquors, exert their muscles for their own good, at the cost of public interests and safety. "Guns do not kill, people do," therefore, there is no need to control gun sales or do background check.

Tobacco lobbies have worked hard to get subsidies for tobacco farmers. Petroleum lobbies can push their interests. Other lobbies like the AMA (American Medical Association) exert their influence. Lobbying may pass as a democratic process, or may be guised as one. However, any lobbying that goes beyond protecting the public good, goes against the public interest, and pushes for its own good is not democratic, and it should be banned.

7. Public Opinion and Interest

The public opinion matters a great deal to the capitalist businesses and institutions. It used to be that they could learn of the public sentiments and act accordingly. That has changed into a public relations showmanship. Rather than respecting the public opinion, attempts are made to show, just show the public that all along, companies have been doing what the people wanted.

Public wants progress? Show them the smoke stacks bellowing dark clouds. Do they want jobs? Show them a Black man and a White woman working. Environment is in vogue? Show a pair of swans near an off shore oil well.

Feed the public the lies, the half lies, and nothing but the lies, even after they have been showed conclusively to be lies. Repeat them ad infinitum in the media, with louder and louder voices to drown out the nucleus of truth and semblance to decency.

Instead of truth and valid arguments for or against any position, fill people's minds with mud, half-truths, and fear of various kinds without any connection to the reality.

The idea is to confuse people and cause a mental fatigue and haplessness, leading to apathy and inaction. Draw public attention to others and put the blame on them. Banks are broke? President Clinton made them do the risky lending. When is the last time they listened to a President anyway?

The worst part is, the friends of capitalism and big business are using all means of communication to obfuscate the problems and to prevent the enactment of laws that are clearly in public interests. If those laws do pass, repeatedly try to undo them, or drag the matter to the highest court.

8. Public Institutions

In addition to the democratic public institutions like the Congress, the Supreme Court, and the Presidency, there are public hospitals, clinics, schools, prisons, and jails, too. There is the Postal Service as well. Many of these came about as public necessities. We talked about the postal service before.

There is lot of confusion about the role of public institutions, including the question, "Whether they should exist at all?" That question comes up because the public not-for-profit institutions do not make profits, but cost some instead. Was not that the definition of those institutions?

Let us understand this clearly. Not all ventures and services are going to generate profits. There are many essential services which nobody wants to provide, and which would have to provided for by someone. There are security nets that are required as a last resort for desperate people.

These services will never be provided by profit-minded businesses. They are not there to provide charitable services, we are told. It may be so, but somebody will have to pick up the slack. Government is responsible for watching all people's interests, and everything falls on its head, whatever no one else would pick up.

Understand this clearly: the government is doing what the businesses would not. Therefore, these public institutions, money-losing by definition, are there to help the people, and businesses that can enjoy their profits.

The public hospitals were created to take care of people without families, income, or insurance. The capitalists would have nothing to do with them. There was no money there. When many of the poor were able to get the health insurance, and the seniors and disabled got Medicare, the private sector suddenly fell in love with these patients.

Smelling the possibility of competition and loss of potential income, complaints against public hospitals started pouring in ("There you go again!"). Their miserable conditions, staff shortage, supposedly poor quality of their physicians and other staff, and so on.

These were especially so for the mental hospitals. Forcing them to send their mentally ill patients, unable to take care of themselves, with hardly any family support, saved some money for the States, and created a big army of homeless people. They would shuttle between prison and mental hospital, without being adequately treated by either. They were too sick for the prison, too criminal for the mental hospitals.

These hospitals have many highly dedicated staff members. I have seen them follow every little progress or regress of their patients. These staff members are poorly paid from a fixed amount, while in the private facilities the hospital, doctors, lab, and pharmacy all will bill separately, and receive several times as much in remuneration.

Private sector wants none of these poor patients, they want the government to take care of them. When there is money to be doled out, the private sector gets interested. At all other times they keep on continuing the demeaning, demoralizing, and untrue attacks on them. They work to destroy the public facilities, take over some of their lucrative business, and leave the rest in the dust, without any provision for any kind of well-thought-out care.

9. The Nonprofit Institutions

Institutions working to help others rather than making profit may appear to be an anachronism in a capitalist country. Instead of making and collecting money, why would anyone give it away? Giving to charity may apparently work to pacify the guilt by supposedly helping the poor. On first look, the nonprofits should not be in this work on capitalism.

Nonprofits do make profit, a lot of it. They use capitalist methods to raise funds. They get money from the well to do and spend it to help the not so lucky ones. There are many intermediaries in their management, some of whom make millions of dollars a year in salaries. They have huge program costs for generating money.

They do not pay taxes. Most of these are genuine charitable institutions of high repute. Many hospitals and religious organizations use their tax-exempt status in creative ways to help their donors save huge amount in taxes.

Nonprofit hospitals take services of volunteers who give them willingly to earn credit for community services. Hospitals require them to have a medical clearance and a few vaccinations, and instead of paying for which, they require the volunteers to bear the expense. These are school students making very little money, if any. This is voluntary slavery and exploitation of the helpless.

Religion and State have been separated by the Constitution. State cannot interfere with religion, which is a personal matter between the follower and God. It should follow, or it should have followed that the church cannot interfere with the matter that are in the domain of the States.

Churches of various denominations use their authority and power to influence the working of the legislature and the President, beyond the matters of interest to the respective religions. Since the religious institutions are nonprofit, tax-exempt organizations, this amounts to creating a strange situation of "representation without taxation."

Promoted to Slavery

Exploitation of volunteers by the nonprofits is not unique. Slavery goes under many euphemisms. Apprenticeship and internships are other tricks, and training is still another. Externship, observerships, etc., are additional disguises for getting free labor. I had undergone internship in hospital, at meager stipend. The pay was called a stipend, rather than salary, because I was supposedly in a training program. Nurses got more than what I got.

Externships are free services extracted from unemployed physicians awaiting their exam results or a residency. There is no restriction on the number of externs that a training program can recruit. These externs are not paid any stipends either, and are required to pay for their own meals, etc. Some prestigious programs even extract a fee for the privilege of working there.

Some of these arrangements are open ended, running for years at a stretch, with no guarantee of getting an internship in that facility. Some programs do make this point clear at the outset, though. The candidates still work there to gain some "work experience," hoping to improve their chances of landing an internship.

They are victims of the capitalist greed of the organized medicine. The latter wants to keep the number of active doctors low, and therefore, keeps on putting obstacles in the path of these fully trained doctors, many with years of private practice and professorships in their countries of origin.

Training programs for lawyers, accountants, etc., also have such requirements to provide help to the businesses at the expense of the neophytes. There is no reason, why these employees cannot be hired at a lower level for the first few months.

One would imagine that once you become a full-fledged lawyer, or doctor, or an engineer, the "voluntary" free labor ends. In a way it does, to come back in a different guise, that of a middle manager. These are the employees who are promoted to a higher pay scale after several years of seniority.

They may interview new candidates for the job, can administer internal training programs, prepare various reports, and carry titles like, "vice president," "coordinator," or "Assistant Director." However, they do not have any hiring or firing powers, nor do they handle the department budget.

What do they get? In addition to the title and somewhat higher pay, they become part of the management, as opposed to be part of the labor force. They continue to do their same labor jobs, but now they become ineligible for the overtime pay. Their number of working hours has no upper limit. They work on weekends, often from their homes. You see some of them checking their e-mails on the beach (the rest are just workoholics or showoffs).

These workers have no job protection. They have no meaningful union strengths. They can be fired or laid off for no cause. In one hospital where I was one of the Assistant Directors of Medicine, nine employees were let go on the Fourth of July weekend (as if to celebrate the Independence Day). The hospital lost the court case and had to rehire eight of them, except myself, who was considered a manager, although I did the same work as they did.

***

Is Capitalism Good for America?

Capitalism, democracy, and America go together in the minds of people at home and in the world at large. Success of America is that of democracy and capitalism. Millions of people from all over the world come to America, many among them risking their lives. America is a rich, free, open country that all its residents, that is we, should be and are proud of.

It has been said about democracy that it is a lousy system of government, but that is the best one around. The same statement has been used after substituting "capitalism" for "democracy." What makes democracy the best available system of government is its accommodation for dissent, its willingness to dialogue, its admittance of likelihood of being imperfect, and its desire to improve.

Capitalism has not shown any tendency to do any of these. It has worked to maximize profits, pampered greed, has not shown any concern for people at large, their institutions, or their government. Assuming it is good for us, their definition of "us" is not the "US" and its people. If the latter have received any benefits, they are tangential, and incidental. In fact, it receives lot more from people than it gives.

Capitalism did serve the country well before the country was completely populated and occupied, and its natural resources were thought to be infinite. The market automatically grew to accommodate and absorb new products and increased production. They did not mind planned obsolescence, when their incomes were increasing, and unemployment was low.

The times have changed. Large capitalist corporations have complete control of the government and the media. Large amount of money controls the election campaigns. Peoples' votes have no value, except to legitimize the wrongs done by corporations. Candidates for public offices pledge their support or otherwise to a cause, before the election, indicating that they are bought out by the private interests.

The Jewish vote, especially in California and New York is crucial in any Presidential election. It is small in number, but large in money. My problem is not with the Jewish people, but rather with our candidates and electoral system. There is nothing more pathetic than our candidates for our highest office debating with each other as to who has been the closest friend with the prime minister of Israel. The latter is our ally, and we do want to stand by it but we cannot surrender the outcome of our elections to it.

Our candidates are falling like sticks (Sorry, for a bad simile, since they have no spines) to various churches, synagogues, temples, businesses, unions, and innumerable lobbies. None of our candidates have the strength or desire to give his or her independent opinion, and vote in favor of the people.

What kind of democracy is this, wherein 99% of the people have to march in the streets, or to "occupy the Wall Street," while 1% can ignore them, the police works to disrupt them, and members of the Congress are too timid to support them?

Our government, I repeat, "our" government will bail out banks and others, but not us. Our House of Representatives will continually work to cut down the unemployment benefits, while opposing any attempt at job creation by the government supposedly for the people.

We want to export democracy to all corners of the world. "Exile" would be a more appropriate term for sending out something that has not been allowed to function here. Democracy has been reduced to a dictatorship of the rich, with an apparently tacit approval by the people. This may be a contributing factor to dwindling voter turnouts and their electoral apathy.

Capitalism and the greed may appear to serve well the interests of the rich. They and a few others may think so, but that is not quite true either, as we shall see towards the end of this work.

***

Is Capitalism Good for the World?

After seeing the socialism and the communism fail, the rest of the world is interested in capitalism and its benefits. They see the progress, high standard of living, and better job situation. They also see the democracy working in America for nearly two and a half centuries, and peaceful transfers of power.

Among the benefits of democracy, come the human rights, women's equality, unrestricted education, and the freedom of speech, expression, and belief. To some of the old timers and religious leaders abroad, these are seen as perversions of a devilish Western culture.

The Middle East, Africa, and Asia are the potential new markets for the American goods, and the American business and government are eager to help them with their dreams. There is a great deal of mutual mistrust for several easy to understand reasons.

Exporting or exiling our version of democracy to the third world is looked upon with bewilderment. In many countries there are dictatorships, or monarchies, or the likes. These do not care for democracy, and their rulers are happy with their positions. They have lot of wealth generated from exporting their oil to America. They are capitalist, and treat their migrant workers like slaves.

Many more are democracies in the name only, or are precariously perched. They switch between people power and military power. These are very much divided, and directionless. They are small, extremely poor, and without a significant infrastructure.

Their officers hold their posts for a short while before being dethroned by a rival. They have to make quick money while they have the chance. They are susceptible to bribing by the multinational corporations, who can buy many such officers and in return, get whatever they want.

These officers are probably capitalists, since they care more for themselves than anything else, and they do not care at all for their people. These officers give a free rein to the multinationals to dump their toxic waste, cart away the raw materials cheaply, set up manufacturing facilities that ignore all environmental and labor laws, if there are any. The companies are given special tax breaks and special considerations in acquiring land and other resources, in preference to the local population.

Laws are modified to allow the multinationals to sell their goods locally at high price, to compel the governments to stop protecting the local merchants and industries, and to force the latter out of business. Agricultural lands are taken over for setting up factories, making the farm workers unemployed, and a selected few farm owners very rich ex-farm-owners.

One farm supports several worker families that are not able to do any other kind of work. When the farm is sold for exorbitant looking sums of money, the farmer gets unbelievably rich, something he does not quite know how to handle, and may blow away the riches in a short while.

The farm workers are not ready or fit to work in factories, and have to move out to villages, since the city is losing its agrarian base, when people from villages are moving to the cities. In short, there are no jobs. Many workers, thousands of them commit suicide every year.

Farmers do not get much help either. If they decide to continue farming, rather than selling out, they do not get any help from the corrupt government. Without bank loans, they have to fall prey to loan sharks, and being unable to pay them back, they also end up killing themselves in droves.

Then there are the real democracies with proper and regular elections. They are eager to progress, but their idea of progress is limited to the skyscrapers, high-speed railways, and highways. These governments are capable of watching and protecting the interests of their people, but they find visible progress more important to win the re-elections.

Multinationals bring the shining progress, make profits, and take them home, or use that to buy more influence, including the media. The latter keep showing the progress and drown out all the grief. Everybody looks very happy. Nobody understands why farmers and others are dying in droves, by thousands every year.

What does the country get in return? The progress. It does not get any taxes, loses some to concessions, loses precious land, loses agricultural production, gets environmental pollution, and maybe some imported toxic materials. Who is going to clean up after the progress? We shall see. If people are upset, they go to the local government that is unable or unwilling to do anything. Multinationals are not reachable in any case.

The education is privatized. The private schools give better education at a price that few can afford. The poor break their backs to send their kids to these English-medium schools hoping for a brighter future. Government gives up its important mandate. Globalization, privatization, and open and free markets result in removing the governments and giving complete control to the multinationals, with no obligations on their part.

These multinationals are directly and indirectly supported by the International Monetary Fund (IMF), and the World Bank, which are effectively under control of the USA, and can compel the nations to accept all kinds of conditions favoring the multinationals at the cost of the interests of the local people and their government.

Many of the lands taken over are tribal lands, leaving the tribes to abandon their parental lands held in the families for the ages. The tribal people are not able to move in and mix with the other more civilized people, and they find themselves in strange environment with strange people and customs, and are unable to find any work. They are not strong enough even to say "ouch!" It does not matter, because if they did say "ouch," no one would have paid any attention to it.

This new arrangement with the multinationals works like the rehash of the colonial days, when the colonial lords took the raw materials, and dumped the processed goods to the detriment of the local businesses. The lords assumed no responsibility. The only difference is, in the colonial period the foreign ruler set up the government and did put in railways and other services, maybe, for its own benefits.

In the new arrangement, the people's government remains as a shell and a puppet, unable to do anything to help its people, and the multinationals cannot be bothered with.

In a way, the government and people both become slaves of the multinationals. Many countries invite these companies and voluntarily become slaves, but slaves, nonetheless.

Cheap Outsourcing

Telemarketing and software developing jobs are exported from the USA to countries like India where there is no shortage of English-speaking workers. The Customer Service Desks thus manned by trained people come under attacks by the dissatisfied customers from the US that these workers speak poor English. They are doing their best, and their English is only as poor as the American English must have felt to the British people. It is not poor, it is only different, just as the American English is from the Queen's English.

For the software companies, recruiting workers from India minimizes their downtime, since the work left incomplete at the end of the day in the US, can be completed across the globe, while the US staff is asleep. There has been no problem with this, and the Microsoft and other tech corporations went to the Congress to open up the visa for these workers to facilitate their migration. That would have been a move towards free and open markets.

Some of the exported jobs are menial, not wanted by anybody in the US, or the companies just wanted to save money. These employees are paid a wage that is higher than the local rates, thereby causing inflation, and are much lower than the US rates, to cause dissatisfaction among workers. The rates rise further, and the advantage to the companies disappears.

The new markets are hungry for many American products. There are American terminal industrial products headed for the toxic waste dump or a recycling plant, are exported to other countries that either use them as such, or process them, or recycle them, sending the rest to the uncontrolled piles of toxic waste, its fate undecided but its effects well known.

So, the governments and people abroad become the slaves of the multinational corporations. The country's interests are not considered al all. They are in a rapidly moving carousal, in daze of progress, but are not going anywhere at all. The US government helps these corporations, apparently unaware of the damage being done to its own people for which it exists. They are losing in corporate income taxes, and in the balance of trade, as the goods made abroad come to the US as import.

Free Trade:

Various international free-trade agreements practically imposed upon poor and developing countries compel the latter to accept goods that the multinationals dump on them at a price that is too high. These countries cannot encourage or protect their local businesses against this invasion. Privatization goes hand in hand with globalization and free trade. In poor countries, privatization is nothing other than privation. People cannot afford private schools, while the public schools are ignored and are left to deteriorate and die.

Enforcement of the copyright laws prevents local companies from producing medicinal and other products inexpensively. Companies try to patent local remedies used for hundreds of years and thereby deprive the local poor from using them. Protecting the intellectual property rights takes precedent over all rights of the humans.

Free trade in poor countries amounts to giving complete freedom to companies to dump toxic waste, and products of their choice, regardless of local needs, and freeing the companies from any responsibility towards the local population.

It would be fair to expect free migration of people from one country to another. That is however not included under free trade. America closely and understandably guards its borders.

It has been openly said in these countries that globalization, privatization, and free trade are nothing but an excuse to extend the capitalist control over the Asian and African countries. These policies create an illusion of progress on the surface, leaving poverty and misery underneath. They take away the rights, jobs, and lands of the people there, and convert those places into an uncontrolled toxic wasteland. They give no real benefits like the know-how to those countries.

Is Capitalism Good for Our Planet?

It is human to be greedy. That does not necessarily make it humane to be so. Social thinkers and religions have considered greed and gluttony as major sins. Progress for the sake of progress is running into an abyss. The definition of progress varies from person to person, and from country to country.

Material progress vis. a vis. the inner or the spiritual progress is an old argument. The former creates wealth and visible happiness in this birth, while the latter promises happiness in the next birth, at the cost of suffering in this one. The latter has not shown any real gains for the humanity and has degenerated into hypocrisy, and generated a plethora of temples and Yogis, together with confused and deprived people, lost in complicated and contradictory scriptures claiming all kinds of successes. They have kept the poor from waking up, while the material progress has made some very rich, but has also kept most of the people from rising up.

The spiritual capitalism led by religions makes a common cause with the material capitalism, to ensure for people, a miserable existence in this world. Both sides talk a lot about human rights of various kinds. Right to equality, education, various freedoms, and so on. Neither side has addressed the basic human needs like jobs, shelters, and health.

Spiritualists are busy meditating, and do not want humans to have any needs (if the latter still do, in spite of the preaching) while the materialistic capitalists are making sure that the latter are not met. The capitalists resting their entire structure on a base element like greed, have failed to create adequate jobs or housing, and have fought healthcare reforms and other programs helping the poor.

I am a nominally religious person, and I like the religion and philosophy. I am happy to see many religious institutions addressing human needs, however, a majority of them are just a burden on the backs of poor and ignorant people whom they confuse and exploit. These institutions are the best examples of the worst kind of feudalism.

Capitalism thrives on dissatisfaction with the status quo, on greed, on maximizing everything, on creating new products, on mechanical mass production, on planned obsolescence, and on new markets at home and abroad. Its sole purpose is profit. It minimizes costs of raw materials, of production, of labor, and maximizes sale price. It has no regards for depletion of natural resources, environmental pollution, human health and safety, employment, or rights of poor people to have their governments watching their interests.

I have kept this section small, because lot of wasteful philosophizing has been done on this topic. The materialists have not respected basic human values, while the spiritualists have only complained against the materialists, have described the human values in great details without doing anything to help the masses achieve them.

The materialists are intoxicated by their profits and nothing else seems to matter to them, and the spiritualists are deep into their lofty thoughts, but neither have really shown any care for or desire to help the poor, for whom the kind of system matters far less than what that system actually does for them.

Wealth in supposedly spiritual India, for example, resides in a few

Ashrams, innumerable temples, with several Gurus, and in the Swiss bank accounts of the corrupt politicians. All these work to lead their people from the burden of the material greed into the liberation, by surrendering their wealth to the spiritual and political charlatans.

***

Conclusion

Any economic system should be for the benefits of the people, not just a handful, but of all people. It cannot be equally good for all, but it should try to address concerns of all people the best it can. It may ignore the interests of people of other nations, which it probably should not either, but it cannot ignore the concerns of the people of its own country.

A good economic system works for the people rather than for its own good, at the expense of that of people and their government. It can influence the public opinion and the government to an extent, but it cannot and should not muzzle the voices of the people, and take over the control of the government.

We are told that the capitalists are running businesses, not charities. They are interested in making profits, and should not be encumbered with social obligations. This may be true as far it goes, but little thinking shows that this position is not sustainable. If capitalism has no social responsibilities, it is irresponsible. Its purpose is people's benefit, all people's benefits, that is, that of the society, not a very small fraction of it.

It should pay its reasonable and fair share of taxes due and act in the interest of the country. It should not export jobs abroad to increase its own profits or to threaten the unions. It should not try to bypass the environmental protection laws, consumer protection laws, or those against child labor by going abroad.

It should not export its toxic waste or toxic waste production abroad with the help of the corrupt and bribed members of the foreign governments. It should work with foreign governments to further the interests of their people to the extent it can, while helping its own profit motive at the same time.

We have been told repeatedly that capitalism is good for America, it has served us well, and it is the best system around, no matter how imperfect it may be. Just as other underdeveloped nations are awed by the so-called superficial progress, we Americans are brainwashed by the capitalist system, and are unable to see that capitalism has not really kept its implied promise of being good to America.

Capitalism is an old relic from the colonial era, set up to protect the feudal interests. It was honestly and sincerely welcomed by the founding fathers who genuinely saw nothing wrong with it. The system did serve the country while the natural resources were aplenty, and the population was growing.

Equal or Complementary?

Our country is based on the proposition that all men are created equal. All babies are born equal, but not all will become the Presidents of the USA. Potentially, they all can. Subsequent to their births, the equality quickly fades away. In a mature society, the idea of equality needs to be looked at again.

Let us take a parcel of 100 acres of land, on which two families live, each owning 50 acres. That is equality. Let us say, one of them acquires 10 more acres, the other can do the same, and reestablish equality. Now their properties reach a riverfront, with no more land left to buy. If one of them wants more land, (s)he will have to take it away (buy, borrow, or steal) from his or her neighbor.

Let us try to visualize this scenario. When there was ample land available, they could remain equal by each one buying more of it. When there is not, a peculiar situation occurs. When one gets more land, the other has to lose that. This is reciprocity, or the "zero sum game." When one gains, the other has to lose.

Mathematically, the total land is constant, therefore, $A + B = K$. It is obvious that in this situation, when the value of A increases, that of B has to decrease, and vice versa. A and B complement each other, as long as the amount of the total land is fixed.

In the colonial America, with ample land available, we could talk about equality. Today, with the country nearly fully occupied, we have reached the stage of reciprocity, or give and take. Not realizing, or appreciating, or acknowledging this change, has sent capitalism astray.

We have to realize that maximization by one leads to minimization by several others. In order for one to become rich, many have to become poor. "I earned it with my hard work, and I would not share it with anyone else," effectively loses its foundation. Lack of understanding of this reciprocity makes the capitalists claim exemption from all social responsibilities, moral, ethical, or financial.

In light of this, it follows that non-interference by the government in the capitalist system is, at best nonsense, and at the worst, hypocritical. Not to interfere with the markets should not be confused with giving the merchants a free rein. Government has to protect the interest of its people, and has to remove any interference in its path.

Another question is, are the markets really free? We do not have the custom of printing the manufacturer's suggested price (MSP) on products. The consumer has no idea, how much price is reasonable. "Whatever the markets will bear" is a meaningless phrase, if the consumer has no basis to decide how much (s)he should bear. A patient going to a doctor's office does not know what procedure at what price would be right for him or her.

When the big corporations are running the show, how can we assume that the markets are free? It is easier to stand up to the City Hall, than up to these gigantic corporations. They can bully an average consumer into bearing anything.

With decreasing resources and increasing population, when America entered the period of reciprocity, capitalism felt constrained. Being unable to expand, it introduced planned obsolescence, and a new phenomenon called, anti-consumer-ism (as opposed to the anti-consumerism), in which customers were cheated in one way or another. You have to rob others to maximize your gains.

Europe reached this stage long ago, and hence, it was more receptive to Socialism and Communism. Their versions of welfare states and social democracies are thriving quite well in the Scandinavian countries. America will have to move towards some kind of controlled capitalism, it seems.

Capitalism also needs to be reminded that it thrives on consumerism, and it is counterproductive for it to get into an anti-consumer mode, and expect the things to get better. Also, if there is any thinking capacity or desire left, it would be obvious to it that all consumers are employees of someone, and laying off employees is a suicidal move.

One laid off employee, in a chain reaction, removes at least ten consumers from the marketplace. Therefore, it makes sense to re-hire one to bring back ten consumers, and stop complaining about market recovery without consumer spending. Stock market is not a consumer market.

Capitalist entities fought for protecting the banks and others at the expense of taxpayers, created unemployment instead of jobs, and worked to prevent the government from creating any, and to cut down the unemployment benefits mercilessly.

The capitalists have incessantly and inexorably fought to cut taxes, and obtain tax breaks for the rich, claiming that the latter are the job creators even though they do not create any. They are not there to spend their money just to keep the nation's nation's economy going.

It bought over the elections, candidates for various public offices, and stymied the President in executing the healthcare reforms, and financial bailout. This is very disconcerting in the present context. Our government is the only governing body that can make laws to control the abnormal capitalist instincts. If it cannot, or would not, under capitalism's undue influence carry out its duty, then one has to wait for a revolution or a messiah.

European capitalism was seriously threatened by the communist upheaval. It was a labor class movement. It was violent, and it failed to provide a new order that worked in the long run. Should a revolution came now, it will come from the 99%. The "Occupy Wall Street" movement was only a pilot project, and a warning to the entrenched interests. There is an across the board disenchantment with capitalism, in the labor class as well as the huge middle class.

I am not advocating any such occupation of anything. As I mentioned in the preface, any claim by me, or any accusation against me, that I am anti-capitalist is not tenable. I think, capitalism in its current form is unacceptable, but it can be modified to be of any help to itself and to the nation.

Is capitalism good for America? Not for its people at large. What about at least some people? It is apparently good for a very small fraction of people, but that also only apparently. They have become rich and powerful, but their social sense of responsibility, justice, and fairness has been skewed. They are oblivious to the plights of the millions around them. They have become the new slave lords, or colonial masters, converting the rest of the country into their colony.

It is almost anti-American to say anything against capitalism, because it is our system, and is supposedly best one for us. Many of us still keep on saying this, as if to convince ourselves, even after the facts clearly show that it is not so. Capitalism has shown anti-American behavior and it needs to be put in its place. It is not our system, and it has not worked for us, but rather it has worked against us, and our government.

There is nothing, either in our Constitution, or in the writings of any economists that I have read, which prevents us from criticizing the capitalist system. The capitalists love to resort to their favorite game of name calling, every time the going gets rough. They call any attempt at criticism to be "communist," "socialist," "backward," and "liberals," and are not at all "conservative" in their this pursuit.

It has ignored the moral, ethical, and environmental responsibilities, and has tarnished the reputation of America in the world. It has not worked to further the cause of human rights. It has consistently refused to assume any responsibility to do anything.

Is capitalism good for the world? We have been telling them it is, but we have seen that it is not. If it is not good for us, we have no business exporting it. Its expansion into the rest of the world has supported dictatorships, undermined democracies, dumped our toxic waste on them, used their child labor, ruined their farm lands and small businesses. It has created a few novo rich but has created a huge class of poor and unemployed.

It has created increased inflation overseas by outsourcing, and made the poor even poorer. The gap between the "haves" and "have-nots" has increased. Farmers and others have been driven to suicide, by thousands. It has thwarted the real progress.

If capitalism is not good for America and not good for the world, it cannot be good for the planet. The planet's environment is threatened or ruined. Moving toxic products from one country to another does not improve the environment. Capitalism grows like a giant cactus tree in Arizona. It spreads its roots deep and over a huge area in which nothing else can grow. It sucks up resources, labor, freedom, everything from all over the planet, and concentrates in a very tiny place, and the capitalist lords sit on these riches like the proverbial dog in the manger.

Capitalism's success and glory have not been analyzed closely with an open mind. The rest of the world has been attracted by its apparent success and glitter, and is craving for that success and glitter, scarcely realizing the costs in human values, and environmental risks.

If the capitalists are slaves to their greed, the rest of the world has fallen slave to its envy for all the success it is supposedly missing out. All have become slaves, maybe, inadvertently, on their own will at least to start with, and then the process has become autonomous.

The entire planet has, as if, become a giant slave ship. Its human cargo, its crew, as well as its captain, all are slaves, either to their greed or to their envy. The ship does not appear to be in search for freedom, but is rather headed into oblivion. A little thought, a little planning, a little compassion, a little soul searching, may still salvage it.

*** *** ***

BOOKS BY
BHARAT S. SHAH, M.D.

Sanskrit: An Appreciation without Apprehension
(Includes "A Crash Course to Learn the Devanagari
Script,"). Our bestseller on the internet $24

An Introduction to Jainism $15
(Second edition. Our bestseller on the internet) $18

A Programmed Text to Learn Gujarati
(Second Edition) $20

A Crash Course to Learn the Gujarati Script $3

A Crash Course to Learn the Devanagari Script
 (Used for Sanskrit, Hindi, and Marathi languages)
(Second expanded edition 2013) $6

English for the Grandma (In Gujarati) $15

Dawn at Midnight (A documentary novel
on awaiting a liver transplant)   *$12*
(Kindle E-**book)** $5

Sameepe (A documentary popular novel, in Gujarati,
the original version of "Dawn at Midnight."
Not available on Internet. Please Email the author) $10

My Life with Panic Disorder
(A documentary novel) $10
(Kindle E-book) $6

Questions Answers Exclamations:
From the Garage of a Clinical Researcher
(Author's ideas for medical research being
bequeathed to the future generation). $15
Capitalism, colonization of America, and
The Mating Habits of the Praying Mantis $8
(Kindle E-book) $5

Slave Ship Earth:
The Ultimate Triumph of Capitalism   *$8*
Kindle E-book   (In future) $3

All these books are in English, unless noted otherwise.
They are available from amazon.com. Their detailed
descriptions, cover images, sample pages, readers' reviews,
comments, and shipping information, are available on
website of amazon.

For more information, E-mail the author at
<bhrtshah@yahoo.com>

***